John Samuel

The Rochdale pioneers

John Samuel

The Rochdale pioneers

ISBN/EAN: 9783337726508

Printed in Europe, USA, Canada, Australia, Japan

Cover: Foto ©ninafisch / pixelio.de

More available books at **www.hansebooks.com**

TRACTS
FOR THE
TIMES.

❧

Co-Operation---The Only Hope For American Wage Earners.

❧

Sketches of Remarkable Co-Operative Societies Organized by Working-Men under the Pressure of Hard Times and Extreme Poverty

❧

No. 1,

The Rochdale Pioneers,

BY

JOHN SAMUEL.

ST. LOUIS, MO., U. S. A.

THE PIONEERS' CENTRAL STORE.

TRACTS FOR THE TIMES

➤➤➤ ‹‹‹‹

CO=OPERATION==The Only Hope For American Wage=Earners.

➤➤➤ ‹‹‹‹

Sketches of Remarkable Co-Operative Societies
Organized by Working-Men under the
Pressure of Hard Times and
Extreme Poverty.

➤➤➤ ‹‹‹‹

All experience hath shown that mankind are more
disposed to suffer while evils are sufferable
than to right themselves by abolishing
those forms to which they have been
accustomed——*Declaration
of Independence.*

➤➤➤ ‹‹‹‹

Co-Operative stores are breaking down the hard
lines between the section of society which
possesses property and the section
which does not possess prop-
erty--*Goldwin Smith.*

➤➤➤ ‹‹‹

I look on Co-Operators as the Salt of the Working Men.—*Charles Kingsley.*

➤➤➤ ‹‹‹‹

——BY——

JOHN SAMUEL.

CO-OPERATION---The Only Hope of Labor.

"Co-Operation !   ' Tis a wondrous theme—
The patriot effort, the poetic beam ;
Theory and practice here a basis find,
Where the best effort may be well combined ;
To Show the benefits which it may spread
On every hand—to purse, or heart, or head ;
To exhibit it in all its breadth and length,
A moral lever of prodigious strength.
To these great ends I charge you to employ
Your best exertions, and you'll soon enjoy
The peace and pleasure which is bound to flow
From doing good to neighbour, friend or foe.''

TO THE READER.

In the preparation of the following pages the writer has endeavored to keep in view the two-fold objects. First: Showing to American wage-earners what co-operation has done for the improvement of the condition of the working-classes of the old world. Secondly: To make prominent those peculiar features of the Rochdale scheme of co-operation, the social, moral and educational, which have elicited from the most eminent citizens unqualified praise, and given to the Pioneers and their system of the distribution of wealth and its uses, their world-wide fame.

The growing interest in co-operation now manifesting itself here and there, encourages the hope that the apathy and indifference that marked the attitude of American workers towards co-operation twenty years ago, and which proved so discouraging to such earnest and devoted friends of co-operation as the late Josiah Quincy, Rev. Dr. Heber Newton, Rev. Dr. Rylaner, Howard Crosby and others, is passing away.

To aid in increasing and extending this interest should receive the best efforts of all who desire to see co-operation permanently established.

To increase the usefulness of this tract and assist extending co-operation, the reader will find in the Appendix, rules for the government of co-operative societies, with the necessary instructions for forming th same.

A brief notice of the remarkable work done bp woman in co-operation is also given in the Appendix.

—J. S.

CONTENTS.

———

CONTENTS—CONTINUED.

TRACTS FOR THE TIMES

CO-OPERATION---THE ONLY HOPE OF LABOR.

Introduction.

The Panic of 1857==A Forwarner.

When the panic of 1857 swept over this country no sign or warning given of its approach, it left, as the result of its work, destitution and distress in the homes of thousands, that till then had never known the presence of want.

Mills, workshops and factories were suddenly closed, and workingmen by thousands might be seen with dinner pails in hand, not on the way to work, but to the soup houses, opened by the benevolent for the relief of those so suddenly deprived of employment.

The *London Times*, observing the disastrous effects of the panic upon the toiling masses of the country said :—

"'The working classes of America are destined to pass through the same ordeal that the working classes of the old world were passing through.''

A striking and significant comment, and one which the American people, in the light of present industrial conditions, would do well to consider.

THE SCENE CHANGED.

A year later, (1858), an interesting account of a scheme devised by a few workingmen of the Old World, which enabled them to banish from their homes, poverty with its attendant evils, reached this country.

This was the story of the Rochdale flannel weavers and their wonderful success in co-operation, after failing in a strike for an increase in wages, as related by Mr. George Jacob Holyoake, in his entertaining history of the Rochdale Pioneers.

When the history of the Pioneers was published a copy was sent by the author to his friend and co-laborer in social reform, and an earnest advocate of co-operation, Horace Greeley, resulting in an elaborate notice of the Pioneers and their work in the *New York Tribune.*

This was the way that nearly forty years ago, the Rochdale scheme of co-operation that has blessed a million and a half of English working-class homes with comfort and contentment, was brought to the attention of America's highly favored working-classes.

HARD TIMES.

The following graphic description of the times and the condition of England's workers, at the time that the Rochdale Pioneers commenced their work in social reform appeared in the *Co-Operative News,* April 9th, 1893. The writer, Mr. John Kershaw, a coal miner, and one of the original Twenty-Eight members of the Pioneers, at his decease left some interesting papers to be delivered to Mr. Holyoake, containing an account of the origin of the Pioneers Society. Referring to himself in introducing his subject, Mr. Kershaw said he was employed in the mill as a tearboy at seven years of age, and at eight went into the mine.

"The Rochdale Pioneers," he continued, "began their work when the country was suffering from a severe trade crisis. Distress was far and widespread. People were badly fed and badly clothed. The hand-loom weavers seemed to be the worst off of any of the working-class. Improved machinery had driven them to the lowest point at which they could live. In 1840, Mr. Slancy stated in Parliament, that in Liverpool there were 7,860 cellars used as dwellings, inhabited by 30,000 persons, one-seventh of the population of the town. In Manchester and Salford cellar dwelling was as bad. Out of 37,000 houses more than 13,000 were ill-furnished, and 10,000 were without furniture altogether. In Bury things were no better. In 773 dwellings in that town, the families slept three and four in a bed. In 259 houses, there were four and five in a bed, and in fifteen families, six and seven slipt in a bed. Similar reports were made to Parliament from Newcastle-on-Tyne, Leeds and Birmingham. The condition of things in Rochdale would be incredible did it not rest on the authority of Sharman Crawford, the member for the Burough, who declared in the House of Commons in the debate of 1840 that in Rochdale there were thirty-six persons living on 6d. per week; 200 on 10d. per week; 508 on 1s per week; 855 on 1 s. 6d per week; and 1,500 were living on 1s 10d per week. Five-sixths of those he spoke of had scarcely any blankets, eight-five families had no blankets, forty-six families had only chaff beds, with no covering at all. No wonder the country was full of agitation, and in Rochdale where there was intelligence as well as unrest, all agitations seemed to rage. Two social facts stood out very clear: Labor was cheap, but bread was very dear; yet bread was almost the only article of food the people were able to get."

Such, then, were the conditions affecting and
surrounding the lives of the people when the
foundations were laid for a new commercial and
industrial system which subsequently proved
to be the one thing needed to remove the evils of
a false distributive system and substituting
therefor the equitable system devised by the
Rochdale Pioneers.

A STATESMAN'S REMEDY FOR FALSE DISTRIBUTION.

With a clear understanding of the causes
which produced the suffering among the people
just described, an eminent statesman declared
that "no permanent change for the better can
take place in the condition of the working-classes
until they take the management of their own
affairs into their own hands."

CO-OPERATION A FACTOR IN THE WORLD'S COMMERCE.

When the Pioneers had been in business
thirteen years, had increased in members from
28 to 1850, and in funds from $140 to $75,000; had
done business during the period of a *Million and
a Half Dollars*, and divided among its members
in profits nearly *One Hundred Thousand Dollars*,
Mr. Holyoake, in writing up their history, recalling
the words of the statesman quoted, said: "They
have acted on Sir Robert Peel's memorable advice,
they have taken the management of their own
affairs into their own hands, and what is more
to the purpose they have kept them in their own
hands."

The period covered by the first thirteen years
of the Pioneers' operations was the most important in the history of co-operation. It was the
culminating point, reached after years of experi-
ment in efforts to secure for the laborer a firm and
enduring foundation for an equitable system of
distribution, the point where the principle itself
passed from the theoretical or experimental into
the practical, and became a recognized factor in
the world's commerce. It gave to Mr. Gladstone's
argument its greatest force when in his speech in
the House of Commons in 1864, for the extension
of the franchise to the working-classes, pointing

to what the Pioneers had done to justify their claims to the suffrage he said, to quote his words: "For it is in Rochdale where that remarkable system, and at the first sight, I do not hesitate to say, that critical and perilous system obtained of ousting the retail trader, and the working-class taking into its own hand the business of its own supply, and where through an extraordinary intelligence and self-acting power that system has been successfully worked out and made a source of the greatest comfort and profit to the working-class."

Referring to the remarkable progress in co-operation during the preceding decade, 1854-64, he continued: "For I am not ashamed to say, that if ten years ago, anybody had prophesied to me the success of the co-operative system, as illustrated in the towns in the North, if I had been told that laboring men would so associate for their mutual advantage, I should have regarded the prediction as absurd. There is, in my opinion, no greater social marvel than the manner in which these societies flourish, combined with a consideration of the soundness of the basis on which they are build."

Commencing with a few articles of prime necessities, the entire stock in trade at "the opening" costing less than $100, the progress of the Pioneers, and their extension into other lines of business will be seen in the following sketch, and serve, perhaps, to correct a too common error that the Pioneers had no higher object in view than that of saving a few pence in household expenses by buying at wholesale and selling to themselves at retail and pocketing the profits.

In 1847, drapery, or dry goods, was added to the business, and butchering in 1850. In 1851, a capital of $13,000 was raised and a flour mill started to supply the members with pure flour, an article almost unknown to the British consumer in those days, and as rare as pure butter is to the American consumer to-day. In 1852, tailors, shoemakers and cloggers were employed, and in 1855, with a capital of $20,000 a cotton mill employing about forty persons, was in operation.

In a speech by one of the members in 1860, it
was stated that in the productive departments of
the Society, there were then employed eight
butchers, seventeen boot and shoe makers, ten
tailors and ten cloggers; in the corn mill eleven;
in the manufacturing mill, forty-two, making a
total of ninety persons employed by the Society,
not including those employed in distribution.
Another advance made by the Pioneers this year
was the organization of a Land and Building
Society, to enable members to assist each other
in building or purchasing a better class of dwellings than those they occupied. Their first step
in carrying out this enterprise was the purchase
of a plat of land for which $100,000 was paid, and
on which nearly forty cottages were erected.

The following extract from a speech delivered
by the Honorable John Bright in the House of
Commons, this year, indicates the deep interest
felt by a few public men in this new movement
by workmen to better their condition. Rochdale
was Mr. Bright's home and he was in the habit of
visiting the Pioneers at their store for information in relation to their work. In the speech
referred to, he said:

"Now, I shall ask the attention of the House to
a statement respecting the workingmen of Rochdale, I refer to certain associations in the Borrough
of Rochdale, known as co-operative societies,
where workingmen exclusively have created large
mercantile concerns and have managed them for
many years past with the greatest possible success. During the first quarter of the present
year, (1860), its trade was $170,000 and the profits
divided among members amounted to $16,575.
Its establishments consist of a large grocers'
shop, and another, I think, where shoes are sold.
Gentlemen who suppose that these workingmen
are not aware of what is being done and said in
this House, will attach some importance to the
facts I am about to adduce. The Society has a
library and reading room open free to all its
members, who now number 2,900. The library
contains from 3,000 to 4,000 volumes, the reading
room is well supplied with daily and weekly

papers, and monthly and quarterly periodicals, and doubtless some of the members have read the article in the quarterly of which we have been speaking here. Maps, globes, telescopes, &c., are provided for its members, and a sabbath school is attached to the institution."

THE AMERICAN CIVIL WAR AND ITS EFFECT ON CO-OPERATION.

The years 1862—65, inclusive, were among the most eventful years in the history of the Rochdale Pioneers. The blockade of the ports of the Southern States, as a result of the civil war, effectually prevented the exportation of cotton. This, in turn, caused the suspension of most of the cotton mills of England, thereby throwing out of employment about a million operatives. It was among these operatives that co-operation had made the greatest progress.

Such was the effect of the "cotton famine" upon this industry, that by a return made to Parliament in 1863, it was shown, that in consequence of the suspension of work upwards, of 11,000 members of co-operative societies were compelled to withdraw, whose withdrawals from their accumulated savings, amounted to $863,000. In the Rochdale Society alone, the membership dropped from 3,900 to 3,501, with a reduction in capital of 22,300, but by the timely formation of a loan fund by the committee of management to enable members, by the aid of temporary loans, to retain membership, further withdrawals were prevented. The wisdom of this arrangement was soon made manifest. In 1863 there was an increase in members of 514, and in capital of $54,480. During 1864 there was a further increase in members of 732, and in capital of $63,720. During the four years ending December, 1865, the net increase in members in the Rochdale Society war 1,426, with an addition to capital during this trying period to workingmen of $179,265. The increase in trade during the period amounted to $100,140, and in profits $30,680. When thousands

in business were forced into bankruptcy by the
panic, these poverty-ridden workingmen of 1844
were advancing, building new branch stores for
the accomodation of their increasing membership, and disbursing on these and other improvement more than $30,000. To the reading rooms
and library the appropriation exceeded $9,000 and
nearly $4,000 given to relieve the distress result-
ing from enforced idleness.

RESULTS OF THE FIRST TWENTY YEARS
IN CO-OPERATION.

In reviewing the work of the first twenty
years effords in co-operation, the committee of
management in their twentieth anual report re-
mind the members of the origin of the society,
the trials, difficulties and opposition encountered
and overcome, the substantial progress made
during the period reviewed, not only financially
but socially and intellectually for the members
were now receiving free a sheet almanac showing
the progress of the society yearly since 1844; the
sub-heading of which was the "The objects of
the Society are the Social and Intellectual Advancement of its Members." The following
extracts from the report are instructive and its
conclusion hopeful and encouraging

FROM THE TWENTIETH ANNUAL REPORT
FOR 1864. — TO CO-OPERATORS.

Twenty years have now passed away since a
few workingmen in Rochdale, despairing of success in a strike against giant capital for an
advance of wages, resolved to form a Co-operative society, the objects of which were the
improvement of their social and domestic condition. How far these objects have been realized
the tables and other information contained on
this sheet (sheet almanac) will show. That
co-operation is superior to strikes for accomplish-
ing these objects, few will dispute. That it is
more conducive to the happiness of the greatest

number than competition, there is no question. That it will ultimately prove the salvation of the laboring class, there is little doubt. Many have been the predictions at different times that it would prove a failure, and many attempts made to prove the prediction true, but its benefits have been well known, and confidence well grounded. Surely twenty years are sufficient to test its sound ness and prove that if it should fail, it will not be from any defect in its principles. There have been many trials and difficulties to contend with and obstacles to overcome, but a strong conviction in the justness of the cause has conquered them all. Each year from the commencement, except 1862, has shown an increase in capital and members, notwithstanding that we have had to pass through several periods of bad times and scarcity of work. Bad times seem to give impetus to co-operation, for there is always an accession of members when they are over, which proves that the uses of adversity are sweet. Though the cotton trade is still bad, and hundreds who are employed in it, (or should be) are in the greatest distress, our members have increased in the past year from 4,013 to 4,747 and the capital from $246,805 to $310,525. If we take a retrospective glance at the success of the past twenty years, it is indeed gratifying and cheering. When we consider that the aggregate profits of this society alone, amount to $653,865 we must be satisfied that the social and domestic condition of its members are improved. But much as has been done, there still remains much to do. The original programme is not finished. The next twenty years may see co-operation developed in higher forms and the laboring class elevated to a position of independence and happiness never before enjoyed."

Referring to the educational feature, the Report states: "The educational Department has also received great attention, two additional news rooms having been opened—the rooms being specially built for the purpose. The majority of our members have now a news-room at no very inconvenient distance from their

homes, and we hope they will make the best use
of the advantages they afford for intellectual
improvement."

In the Twenty-First Annual Report of the
Society, an extract from which follows, the committee recalls attention to the humble origin of
the society, its remarkable progress in the face
of the panic, and refer with just and honest pride
to the fact that from its inception to its "coming
of age" it was purely and exclusively a working-
man's movement. The committee's intense
solicitude in regard to the educational feature is
again emphasized, and concludes with express-
ing the hope that they would "never again have
such a famine for cotton; or cotton stained with
the blood of the slave."

EXTRACT FROM REPORT FOR 1865.

Twenty-one years ago, Rochdale gave birth
to this Society which has since become so famous
for its progress, and so extensive in the diffusion
of its benefits; and although it was at that time
designated by some; "The Weaver's Dream," yet
it must be a pleasant reflection on the part of
those veterans in co-operation with whom origi-
nated the scheme, to have witnessed the growth
of this somewhat unhealthy child at birth, and
attain its majority with a constitution at once
strong and robust; and while it cannot boast of
having sprung from a titled household or an
aristocratic ancestry, yet it has been proved
since that it possessed the germs of a superstruc-
ture that was destined to eclipse the expectations
of the most sanguine, and to astonish, contradict
and perhaps, disappoint its false prophets.

We do not need to go back to the time when
it commenced to show the sound position it has
attained, but the fact that we have not only main-
tained our existence, but actually progressed in a
remarkable degree in one of the most severe and
longest panics on record, is one convincing proof
of its soundness and of its strenghth." Referring the reader to the figures given of the prog-

ress of the society during the panic, the Report goes on to say: "From these figures some idea may be drawn as to what the society has been doing during the cotton famine. It will be seen that the society has not absolutely and entirely aimed at getting dividend and profit, but likewise the education and improvement of its members, for if there is one feature more than another to which we can look with satisfaction and pleasure, it is the ample provision that is made for the diffusion of every class of knowledge and useful information on all the sciences, arts, and literature of our time. We also entertain the hope that the day is not far distant when schools will be established in connection with the society, to educate the rising generation of co-operators."

OPENING OF THE (NEW) CENTRAL STORES

The twenty-eight of September, 1867, was a notable day in the history of the Pioneers. On that day they moved from their old quarters in Toad Lane, into their new premises, near by, known as the Central Stores, which had been nearly two years in building, erected at a cost including site, or $67,500.

Distinguished friends of co-operation were present and took part in the speech making, among others, R. J. Hilton of Washington.

Mr. Holyoake, in his opening remarks referring to the humble origin of the society, its wonderful progress, the commanding position of the new stores, and the magnitude of its trade, said:

"Twenty-three years before the co-operators had commenced their humble and doubtful career in Rochdale and that day, Sept. 28, '67, they obtained acknowledged ascendency in the town. They had become the greatest trading body extant. Their building stood upon the best site, and towered like Saul, head and shoulders above every other establishment about it."

Rev. W. N. Molesworth, Vicar of Spotland, one of the earliest and warmest friends of the Pioneers, in his address pointed attention to the influence the Rochdale system of co-operation was exerting in other countries when he said:

"He regarded that celebration as of European importance. Throughout the Continent co-operation had spread rapidly since they had adopted the principles of the Rochale Pioneers. All true believers in co-operation turn their eyes to Rochdale as the Mecca and Medina of the system."

Interesting addresses by Tom Hughes, author of "Tom Brown's School-Days," Mr. Walter Morrison, M. P., and members of the Society, followed. The large hall, used as the meeting-room of the Society, with a seating capacity for 1.400 persons, is located on the fourth floor of the building, and affords an excellent view of the surrounding country. The library, news-room and waiting-rooms are below the meeting-room, while the offices of directors, committees, &c., are on the second floor. With an illustrated sketch of the new stores which appeared in the *Co-Operative News*, March 15, 1873, it was shown that in addition to the productive enterprises already mentioned, the Society was carrying on bread, biscuit and cake baking, coffee roasting, and coffee and pepper grinding, currant cleaning, pork butchering and tobacco manufacturing.

Let the reader pause a moment here to consider but one of the above remarkable achievements, taking the essential article of food—bread. With the flour mill and bakery in their own hands, they brought producer and consumer into closer relations by eliminating the miller, the jobber, the wholesaler, retailer and baker; five intermediates that stood between the wheat grower and the wage-earning consumer. Within the short period of thirty years the Pioneers had done for themselves and the public that which was pronounced as impracticable as crossing a trackless ocean in search of a new world. They placed upon the working-man's table a two-pound loaf of pure unadulterated bread for the sum of five cents. This, to the British worker, with a half-dozen mouths to fill, and whose wages ranged from four dollars a week to ten and eleven dollars, is one of the reasons why he so highly appreciates co-operation as an inestimable boon to him and his family. The bringing together the mill and the bakery meant to him a reduction in the price of flour from $13 to $4 a barrel. Let the American reader now turn his attention to this important question as affecting his own condition and that of his family within the last twenty years, and he will perhaps learn with surprise how and why bread is dear to the American consumer. Within that period the murmers of dissatisfaction at the smallness of the loaf, and sometimes the quality of the article, have not been few nor far between. It has been heard with more or less intensity and emphasis in most of our large cities—New York, Philadelphia, Chicago, St. Louis, and other industrial centers. Taking St. Louis as an illustration. In the fall of 1884. the expressions of discontent at the size and weight of the five-cent loaf were so pronounced and widespread as to induce a paper to send out a number of reporters to ascertain the popular feeling on the subject. Large employers in the trade and journeymen, small bakers whose trade was limited, housekeepers and consumers of every kind were interviewed and the interesting information conveyed to the public that in the majority of cases the weight of the five-cent loaf ranged from thirteen to fifteen ounces. At a conference of millers held some years ago, it was stated that a pound of flour of fair quality made a pound and a quarter of bread. Taking this as a basis, a barrel of flour — 196 pounds — would yield 245 pounds of bread, which, at five cents per pound, amounts to $12.25. As shown in the St. Louis' investigation that most of the bakers did not buy the best flour, the article ranging in price from $3.50 to $5. The reader will see the standpoint from which the Rochdale Pioneers studied the problem of production and consumption.

Pure butter was another article the Pioneers rarely tasted until they procured it from first hands. Before they had completed their fifteenth year in business, they had an agent travelling the year round among the dairy farmers of Ireland, (Irish butter holding the leading place in the English market,) purchasing their butter, eggs and other products, paying the producer in cash on the spot, something he had never known done before, and shipping the produce direct to the store at Rochdale.

When the Pioneers brought themselves into direct trade relation with the producer they demonstrated not only the practicability of reducing the cost of distribution at least one-fourth as compared with the cost under the competitive system, but, what is of infinitely more importance to public and morals suppressing effectually the iniquitous practice of adulteraion.

When wheat can be raised for fifty cents per bushel and pure butter placed upon the consumers' table for fifteen cents per pound, producers and consumers should know where the difference goes, when the latter has to pay five cents for a fourteen-ounce loaf and thirty cents a pound for butter.

A POLITICAL ECONOMISTS SHOWS WHERE THE DIFFERENCE GOES.

Replying to a letter from the Secretary of the Association for the promotion of co-operation, informing him of another effort to establish a wholesale agency in London, John Stuart Mill, who was watching the development of the co-operative movement with keen interest, in referring to the subject of the latter, said:—

"The subject of a wholesale agency, which is now occupying the attention of the Society, is one of great importance and I hope it will be found practicable to establish such an agency, both as a great means of saving expense and as valuable extension of the Co-operative principle. It is the enormous number of mere distributors who are not producers that really eat up the product of labor. * * * * * * *

The direction in which I look for for the greatest improvement in social economy is the suppression of the vast number of Middlemen who share among themselves so large a proportion of the produce of the country while the services they render, though indispensable, might be as well and better performed by a tenth part of their number."

Another illustration of the power of co-operation in suppressing adulteration is furnished in the reply of Mr. John Gledhill, representative of the English Co-Operative Wholesale Society to Mr. J. K. Brown, New York State Dairy Commissioner, in the correspondence published in the *Co-Operative News*, February 13, 1886.

Replying to a request from Mr. Brown for information as to "what the experiences of the organization he represented had been in selling oleomargarine, or imitation butter to customers who knew exactly what they were purchasing, Mr. Gledhill, said:—

"The demand for imitation butter on the part of our customers is so small that I seldom hear the article mentioned. The Co-Operative Wholesale Society, which I have the honor to represent, is a federation of about seven hundred Retail Co-Operative Societies of England. The object of the retail societies in thus combining together was to place experienced buyers in the center of production of the various articles in which they dealt. By this means we obtained pure and adulterated commodities at as near the cost of production as ready money can buy them. The Wholesale Society, after buying its goods, re-sells them at the current wholesale prices, to its own share-holders (the Retail Societies) who have a regular outlet for them.   *   *   *   *
As the Wholesale Society caters for no trade outside its own share-holders, there is no temptation to buy bogus butter and resell it to themselves as genuine, as that would be only cheating themselves. If we buy oleomargarine we

re-sell it as such, and probably this honest way
of doing business accounts for the very insignific-
ant trade we have in it. Personally, I have no
objection to the manufacture of oleomargarine,
providing, of course, the article is sold as such
and some law enforced so as to punish dishonest
trades people who sell it for real butter to un-
suspecting customers. Co - Operative Retail
Societies are composed chiefly of what may be
called the thrifty working-classes, who, as a rule,
want the best of everything in the way of
eatables, therefore, the bulk of the Wholesale
Society's trade in butter consists of only the very
finest quality. The total weight of butter sold
for the year 1885 was over 20,000,000.''

When Mr. Gledhill gave Mr. Brown the above
information, the Co-Operative Wholesale Society,
which was then nearing the close of its twenty-
second year, had seven receiving and shipping
departments in Ireland and importing besides
the dairy products of Denmark, Holland. Sweden
and other countries. Its importation of butter,
bacon and eggs from Denmark for the quarter end-
ing June 26, 1897, amounted to $1,830,625; while the
total value of the wheat, flour, bacon, hams, lard,
cheese, etc., received from America during the
same period amounted to but $397,585. The
dairy producing interests of Denmark are almost
entirely conducted on the co-operative principle.
In addition to the enterprises already mentioned,
coffee roasting, coffee and pepper grinding, pork
butchering, tobacco manufacturing, etc., it is
evident that the Pioneers did not mean to stop
half way in the work of reform. They knew,
as well by their own experience, as by the numerous suits brought against unscrupulous dealers
that these things seldom reached the consumer's
table in a pure state; while the ineffectual efforts
of all civilized governments, not excepting our
own, to prevent or regulate, by sanitary laws,
the marketing or sale of unhealthy live stock,
satisfactorily explains why the Pioneers established their own slaughter-houses, aside from
its economic value and importance.

1892 — CO-OPERATIVE CONGRESS AT ROCHDALE.

The year 1892 was memorable in the history of co-operation, as the year in which the Twenty Fourth Annual Co-Operative Congress of Great Britian was held at Rochdale, the birth-place of the movement. A gathering of nearly a thousand delegates representing nearly a million members — the brawn and brain of the wealth-producing forces of the nation, owning, controlling and conducting commercial and industrial enterprises of the greatest magnitude, running up into hundreds of millions of dollars, must have appeared to those delegates in striking contras t to the meeting of the twenty-eight poor weavers, who, forty eight years before, by the slender subscription of four cents weekly from their scant wages, laid the foundations of the movement they were then and there representing.

The opportunity of looking upon the last resting-places of the Pioneers was not allowed to pass unimproved. Among other incidents of the Congress gathering was the visit by many delegates, with Mr. and Mrs. Holyoake as guides, to the grave of John Bright, one of the true and tried friends of co-operation, when friends were few.

In an impressive speech at the grave, on the services rendered by the departed statesman to the people while in Parliament, Mr. Holyoake said, among other things: "The reason why co-operators should pay a visit to this grave is this — that Mr. Bright was the most effective and brilliant defender of co-operation in Parliament. He was the first man who raised his voice there on behalf of co-operators."

In the one hundred years of legislation now passed but one voice has been heard in our American Congress in favor of co-operation as an aid in improving the position of the working classes. That voice was the voice of the late Senator Stanford, when in February, 1887, he introduced a bill to establish co-operative associations in the District of Columbia.

The introduction of that bill was Labor's opportunity. Had organized labor at Washington promptly taken up the measure and pressed upon Congress the necessity and importance of its speedy consideration and passage, there can be little doubt as to the result. The bill would have passed and co-operation secured a legal status at the capital of the nation.

The next step probably, would have been the formation of a co-operative society, and with one hundred members and the necessary amount of capital paid in, a co-operative store started within one year. Had that been the course pursued by organized labor at Washington when Senator Stanford presented his bill there can be little room for doubt that the Society, at the end of ten years, would have had 1,000 members. One thousand workingmen and women trading at their own store at an average of $3.00 each per week, would see, as a result, an annual turn-over of $160,000.00; netting at the low rate of five per cent., exclusive of expense of management, etc., profits amounting to $8,000.00. Workingmen so united and combined and increasing yearly in numbers and wealth would naturally attract the attention of Senators and Representatives, while some like John Bright, curious to know something more about this new movement among workingmen, would visit the store, and, as a result, take back with them on their return home the printed reports of the Society, some of which would probably contain extracts from the senator's speech on introducing the bill, and thus co-operation would be spread from the capital of the nation into every state and territory in the Union.

The remarkable progress made in co-operation twenty years before Senator Stanford introduced his co-operative measure would have justified the belief that co-operation had come to stay.

During the middle and later part of the '60's co-operative stores were in successful operation in many states, Massachusetts leading with from twenty to twenty-five in 1870.

Co-operation was then a leading question in labor reform. A convincing proof of this fact was to be seen in the number of co-operative foundries, W. H. Sylvis was instrumental in establishing. As president of the Iron Moulders International Union, his position as the executive head of his organization gave him peculiar facilities for propagandic work and his able and earnest addresses to workingmen were seldom made without impressing upon them the paramount importance of giving their immediate attention to co-operation as the one sure and effectual solution of the labor question. The effect of Mr. Sylvis' speeches on the necessity of labor organization was felt long after he had passed away, and largely contributed to the spread of co-operative ideas among the masses.

The following extract from Dr. R. T. Ely's valuable work on "The Labor Movement in America," conveys but a faint idea of the wide spread interest manifested in co-operation during this period and it was the impetus given to the principle at this time that lead to its incorporation in the Grange Declaration of Purposes, and the Declaration of Principles of the Sovereigns of Industry and Knights of Labor.

"Whenever co-operation has in this country assumed large proportions," says Dr. Ely, "it has been connected with some trade union or labor organization and those societies, which are to be specially borne in mind in this connection are the following, namely: The New England Protective Union, the Patrons of Husbandry, the Sovereigns of Industry, and the Knights of Labor."

The efforts of these organizations in co-operation and *why* they failed will appear in future tracts. To return to the Rochdale Congress. The marvelous progress of the co-operative movement had for years been winning to its advocacy and support the most distinguished men in Church and State. The following extracts from sermons preached at the Rochdale Congress illustrate the influence exerted by co-operation on the religious mind and thought of the nation

At the conclusion of the morning service at the Free Methodist Church, where the Congress met, Rev. M. F. Myers gave the delegates a warm welcome in the following words:

"We welcome you to Rochdale, and as representing our church and people here, we welcome you to this Chapel in which to hold your business meetings. We are glad to see you here. The time has come, we think, when chapels of this kind ought to be used for purposes of this kind. I thought that when the matter was first suggested to me, we are getting into brighter, better days quickly."

The Rev. B. Veitch, Congregational, in his sermon on the ideal social state, said:

"It was just where difficulties had arisen with trades unions that co-operation came in as a further necessity. Its main object was to secure a more general distribution of wealth among all those who contributed to its production. It sought to combine the interests of capital and labor, of producer and consumer. By this method greater economy and stability were obtained; friction reduced and severe competition restrained. When the producer was united to the consumer and the capitalist to the laborer by common interests, which was sufficiently evident, much of the social warfare destructive of peace and prosperity would have passed away."

"Coming Developments of the Co-Operative Idea," was the subject of an instructive and practical sermon by Rev. J. M. Hollowell, Congregational.

After pointing out that co-operation had a broad, moral basis and began by honoring work, the preacher said that it must, therefore, take other forms than retail purchasing and thought to associate men in buying bread, butter, soap, etc., at one shop was good, so far as it went, it was not a sufficient organization of the community. Wage earners ought increasingly to

BUSINESS MAXIMS OF THE PIONEERS.

To insure the continuance of the work on the lines laid down, and the foundations on which that work was so firmly and securely based, the Pioneers submitted, for the guidance of others, and as the result of their own practical experience, the following:

ADVICE TO CO-OPERATORS.

1st. Procure the authority and protection of the law by enrollment.

2d. Let integrity, intelligence and ability be indispensable qualifications in the choice of officers and managers, and not wealth or distinction.

3d. Let each member have only one vote, and make no distinction as regards the amount of wealth any member may contribute.

4th. Let majorities rule in all matters of government.

5th. Look well after the money matters. Punish fraud, when duly established, by the immediate expulsion of the defrauder.

6th. Buy your goods, as much as possible, in the first markets; or if you have the produce of your industry to sell, contrive, if possible, to sell it in the last.

7th. Never depart from the principle of buying and selling for ready money.

8th. Beware of long reckonings. Quarterly accounts are the best, and should be adopted when practicable.

9th. For the sake of security, always have the accounted value of the fixed stock at least one-fourth less than its marketable value.

10th. Let members take care that the accounts are properly audited by men of their own choosing.

11th. Let committees of management always have the authority of members before taking any important or expensive step.

12th. Do not court opposition or publicity, nor fear it when it comes.

13th. Choose those only for your leaders whom you can trust; then give them your confidence.

The following is the form of the heading, objects
capital; how raised and other information
on the sheet almanac:

ROCHDALE EQUITABLE PIONEERS' SOCIETY, LIMITED.

The Objects of the Society are the Social and Intellectual Advancement of Its Members.

The capital is raised in shares of $5. A person
on becoming a member, must take out not less
than five, nor more than 200 shares, which may
be paid at once, or by installment. After paying
interest on capital at the rate of 4 per cent per
annum, reduction of fixed stock and 2½ per cent
to the Educational Fund, the remainder is divided
amongst the members in proportion to purchases.

The table shows the progress of the Society in members,capital, business, profits for fifty years:

YEAR	MEM-BERS	FUNDS	BUSINESS	PROFITS
1844	28	$ 140	$............	$ ....
1845	74	905	3 550	110
1846	80	1 260	5 730	400
1847	110	1 430	9 620	360
1848	140	1 985	11 380	585
1849	390	5 965	33 055	2 805
1850	600	11 495	65 895	4 40
1851	630	13 925	88 190	4 950
1852	680	17 325	81 760	6 030
1853	720	29 240	113 800	8 370
1854	900	35 860	166 820	8 815
1855	1 400	55 160	224 510	15 530
1856	1 600	64 600	315 985	19 605
1857	1 850	75 710	398 940	27 350
1858	1 950	90 800	360 200	31 420
1859	2 703	135 300	520 060	33 695
1860	3 450	188 550	760 315	79 530
1861	3 900	214 625	881 030	95 100
1862	3 501	192 325	705 370	87 820
1863	4 015	246 805	793 160	98 355
1864	4 747	304 525	874 655	113 585
1865	5 326	393 890	981 170	125 780
1866	6 246	499 945	1 245 610	159 655
1867	6 823	642 175	1 424 550	208 095
1868	6 731	616 165	1 454 500	187 295
1869	5 809	467 115	1 182 190	142 710
1870	5 560	401 455	1 115 105	126 045
1871	6 021	537 500	1 232 610	145 130
1872	6 444	664 560	1 337 885	168 200
1873	7 021	804 430	1 436 060	193 745
1874	7 639	964 070	1 494 440	203 395
1875	8 415	1 128 410	1 528 985	241 060
1876	8 892	1 270 000	1 525 250	253 340
1877	9 722	1 401 375	1 558 770	258 240
1878	10 187	1 461 720	1 693 395	263 470
1879	10 427	1 440 175	1 350 360	248 755
1880	10 613	1 462 850	1 417 275	242 725
1881	10 697	1 510 755	1 360 710	231 210
1882	10 894	1 576 215	1 373 135	238 040

TABLE—CONTINUED.

YEAR	MEM-BERS	FUNDS	BUSINESS	PROFITS
1883	11 050	1 634 375	1 382 280	257 995
1884	11 161	1 647 350	1 311 350	251 340
1885	11 084	1 623 225	1 260 360	226 270
1886	10 084	1 608 390	1 230 155	220 555
1887	11 152	1 640 500	1 283 680	230 235
1888	11 278	1 723 345	1 338 630	235 595
1889	11 342	1 767 350	1 353 425	236 315
1890	11 352	1 811 790	1 352 915	238 820
1891	11 647	1 853 960	1 480 125	260 990
1892	11 884	1 899 470	1 512 270	251 280
1893	11 989	1 794 610	1 451 190	242 870
1894	12 344	1 755 630	1 425 715	243 585

PROGRESS:

December 21, (1844).—Store opened with a small stock of flour, butter, sugar, oatmeal and a few other articles.

(1851).—Butchering department; Corn Mill organized.

(1852).—Shoemaking and Tailoring started.

(1856).—Wholesale Manufacturing, Etc., organized.

(1857).—First Branch Store started.

(1860).—Land and Building Society organized.

(1867).—The Pioneers in their new store costing with the land, $65,000.00

OPINIONS OF EMINENT MEN ON CO-OPERATION.

When the British Association for the Advancement of Social Science met at Manchester, about the year 1867, Lord Brougham, who was then President of the Association and one of the few public men who was watching with keen interest the progress of co-operation, suggested during one of its sessions, an adjournment to enable those who felt interested in co-operation, to visit the famous Rochdale institution.

Rochdale was within twelve miles of Manchester and easily reached by rail within thirty minutes.

It was after this visit and inspection probably, that the noble lord expressed the opinion that:

"Co-Operation was the most important of all the subjects connected with the welfare of the working classes."

J. S. Mill, on the Moral, Mental and Business
Qualifications Essential to the Success of Co-
Operation.

When co-operators became alarmed at the
rapid progress sometimes made in co-operation
and feared a reaction, to quiet these apprehen-
sions, Mr. Mill, said:

"There is no fear that co-operation will go
too far or too fast. It is not an easy thing. If it
had been, people would not have waited until
this period for it. It will advance no farther
than the minds and morals of those engaged
in it, nor faster than honest and competent men
and women can be found to manage its
concerns."

John Elliot Cairnes, Professor of Political
Economy in London University, after reviewing
the many schemes devised to secure to the workers
the full enjoyment of the fruits of their own
labor, said :

"Our reasoning brings us to this conclusion,
that what is known as co-operation—the contri-
bution by many workmen of their savings towards
a common fund, which they employ as capital and
co-operate in turning to profit—constitutes the
one and only solution of our present problem, the
sole path by which our laboring classes as a whole
or even in any large number, can emerge from
their condition of mere hand-to-mouth living, to
share in the gains and honors of advancing
civilization."—Professor Cairnes' Leading Principles," p. 345.

Goldwin Smith came to a like conclusion in
the following words:—

"Co-Operative stores are breaking down the
hard lines between the section of Society which
possesses property and the section which does
not possess property."

Extracts from Senator Sanford's speech in the
United States Senate, February 16, 1887, on introducing the bill to establish co-operative associations in the District of Columbia:

THE VALUE OF CO-OPERATION.

"I believe that co-operation will bring out
the highest capacities of those engaged in it. It
will impart to each individual the stimulous of
knowing that he or she may enjoy the full fruits
of his or her skill and energy in their calling.

THE REMOVAL OF NON-PRODUCERS.

I have the hope and faith that the principles of
our Government, of our Great Bill of Rights, as set
forth in the Declaration of Independence, will yet
pervade the whole civilized world, and as these
ideas are adopted and as they expand into control
of governments, so will disappear great standing
armies; non-producers will be changed into
fruitful producers, adding to the comforts and
happiness of humanity."

THE ADVANTAGES OF CO-OPERATION.

"One of the great advantages of associations
of this kind is that in case of disagreement, death
or failure, the organization goes on, and in this
respect it is freed from the disadvantages of an
ordinary partnership. Besides, the diverse
capacities of the different individuals, whatever
they may be, unite to make up a great whole of
strength and of large capacity."

Very many of the industries would be open
to and managed as well by women in their cooperative capacity as by men !

The moral influences of co-operation are very
great. All in the organization are interested in
the welfare and good conduct of every other
member. All the good influences of the whole
are brought to bear in favor of the individual,
and all the individual members unite to make
the whole most powerful for the accomplishment
of results.

INSTRUCTIONS FOR ORGANIZING CO-ORERATIVE SOCIETIES AND START-ING CO-OPERATIVE STORES.

The idea of starting a co-operative store almost invariably originates with a few thinking, intelligent working-men who have heard or read something of the advantages and benefits derived by workimgmen from co-operation.

An interchange of opinions follows; succeeded by a determination to see what can be done to start a society among the working people there.

Finding the idea favorably received by others to whom it has been mentioned, a provisional committee is formed by the promoters for the purpose of arousing and extending a deeper interest in the subject among the masses.

The first and most important step to be taken by the committee is to obtain all the information on the subject available, to enable them to proceed intelligently in their work.

This information may be obtained by addressing Mr. J. C. Gray, General Secretary of the Co-Operative Union, Long Millgate, Manchester, England, who will forward by return mail a package of tracts, pamphlets, etc., for free distribution. These tracts should be widely circulated among the working classes.

The following extract from one of the publications of the Union will enable the speakers at the meeting to present the objects of co-operation clearly and forcibly:

CO-OPERATION.

A co-operative society enables the working-man to save and to accumulate his savings, merely by buying his food and clothes at his own co-operative shop. He puts the profit of the shop-keeper into his own pocket. Every quarter he is entitled to a dividend in proportion to the amount he has expended at his shop, and those dividends vary from 5 to 15 per cent. Thousands of men in England have, by this plan, been enabled in a few years to save large sums of money, which it would otherwise have been impossible to save. The profits made by these societies for their members are $25,000,000 a year. If the reader of this book asks how he is to become a member, the reply is easy. He should take two or more shares (five dollars each) payable in installments. When a small capital has been thus raised, further shares can be paid by the members out of the quarterly dividend due to them. On every paid-up share he is entitled to *interest* at the rate of five per cent. per annum in addition to his quarterly dividend. There is no other kind of society whereby money may be saved so easily and with so little trouble. All that is wanted for the success of a co-operative society is that the committee of management shall have common sense, give full attention to the business, and select an honest and efficient manager.

Every workingman, by belonging to a co-operative society, not only benefits himself, but he benefits his fellow members. He also prepares the way for improving the condition of his class throughout the country.

The co-operative movement is intended (1) *to place capital in the hands of the working classes,*(2) *to put them in the way of using it to the best advantage for their own elevation. All that is needed is that workmen should everywhere unite and form co-operative societies,this accumulates capital,and then use it so that the workers shall derive the full benefit of their work, after providing for the charge of capital.*

Therefore, *do your duty to yourselves, to your families and to your fellow-workman, and join the co-operative body.*

' Until they do this, there can be no emancipation from dept and dependence, poverty and pauperism. Be your own shopkeepers- and thus become your own employers. Combine, so as to obtain, for yourselves the profits which are now absorbed by others. To put the case briefly, by joining a co-operative society you attain the following advantages:

1. You save money daily, without effort or trouble.

2. Your savings receive larger interest (five per cent.) than you can get with equal security elsewhere.

3. What you buy is never adulterated. It is of the best. It is of the best quality, because you buy direct from the producer.

4. Two and a half per cent. of the profits applied to an "Educational Fund" will enable you, as the society grows, to provide reading-room, library, lectures, and other like advantages for yourself and family.

5. You become a member of a BROTHERHOOD which seeks to bring about great SOCIAL REFORM in the condition of the working classes.

If only half the working-men of this country became members of co-operative societies, they could accumulate funds at the rate of fifty millions a year, which might be employed in the purchase of farms, factories, workshops, mills and mines, and the construction of dwellings. The co-operative societies might thus become large owners of the property of the country, and receive the profits of ownership, by supplying the food, clothes, furniture and other articles required by the population, rich or poor.

To insure success from the start, the trade of 100 members with an average outlay of $3 each per week would be require to meet expenses and pay a dividend at the end of the first quarter. With rigid economy in management and the avoidance of unnecessary expense and waste, this result might be reasonably expected.

It should be noticed here in connection, that co-operation relies solely upon its members and not upon outside trade, for success in business.

In the Rochdale Society profits are distributed quarterly in the following order.

1. Expenses of management.

2. Interest on Loans.

3. Reduction in value of Fixed Stock.

4 Interest on members' capital.

5. Increase of capital for the extension of business.

6. Two and one half per cent. for Educational Purposes.

7. Remaining profits in proportion to trade.

CONSTITUTION

—OF THE—

CO-OPERATIVE SOCIETY.

Article I.—Name and Object.

SECTION 1. This society shall be called the —————Co-Operative Society.

SEC. 2. The object of the society is to elevate the intellectual, moral and financial condition of its members, through co-operative effort, and in accordance with the following plans and arrangements:

1. The establishment of a store to conduct the business of general dealers, wholesale and retail, in food, clothing and other commodities; and to manufacture the same whenever practicable, or when necessary for the employment of such members as may be suffering from an undue reduction of wages.

2. The buying and holding of land and the erection of buildings thereon, for the uses of the Society.

3. To elevate the domestic condition of its members by building or buying suitable homes for such as may need.

4. The purchase or rental of lands or landed estates, to be cultivated by members who may be out of employment, or who may suffer from poor wages.

5. And to proceed, as soon as practicable, to the establishment of a self-supporting home colony, or to assist other societies in establishing such colonies, wherein may be exemplified, in a practical way, the co-operative idea of production, distribution, education and government.

SEC. 3. The office of the society shall be in the city or town of————.

Article II.—Membership.

SECTION 1. This society shall consist of all members who shall have subscribed to these rules, and who own at least one share of the capital stock of the association.

SEC. 2. The application for membership must be accompanied by the recommendation of at least one member of the society, and by the membership fee, which is fifty cents. The name, address or occupation of every applicant for membership must be posted in a conspicuous place in the store of the society at least one week before being voted on by the Board of Directors, whose approval admits to membership. In case of rejection the membership fee shall be returned.

SEC. 3. In case of admission, each applicant shall fully pay up at least the amount of one share before being entitled to the privilege of membership, and shall sign these regulations, which signing shall constitute a contract between the member and the society.

SEC. 4. Every married member agrees to deal at the retail store of the society for those articles of daily use which are laid in of suitable quality and sold at fair ready money prices. The name of any married member who finds it inconvenient to deal to the amount of at least $1.00 per week, shall be laid before the Board of Directors.

Article III.—Officers, when Elected.

SECTION 1. The officers of the society shall consist of a President, Treasurer, Secretary, and eight Directors, who shall serve one year.

SEC. 2. The President, Secretary and Treasurer shall be chosen at the general annual meeting. No person shall be eligible for President who has not been a Director.

SEC. 3. At the first annual meeting of the Directors shall be elected as follows: One-half (4) shall be elected to serve for six months, and the other half for twelve mouths; and thereafter one-half the Board shall be elected at the general meeting in July, and one-half at the annual meeting in January. No member is eligible to the Board of Directors until after six months' admission to the society.

SEC. 4. There shall also be elected at the annual general meeting, three Auditors.

SEC. 5. No employee of this association shall hold office in the Board of Directors, or be an Auditor, under any circumstances whatever.

Article IV.—Duties of Officers.

SECTION 1. The President shall act as Chairman of all meetings of the society, and should he not be present, the members present shall elect one from among them to act as chairman on that occasion. The President, or Chairman, acting in his absence, shall sign the proceedings of the previous meeting. The President shall have a vote on all questions as a member, but shall have no casting vote by virtue of his chairmanship. He shall be a member of the Board of Directors, and shall preside as Chairman, but shall have no vote except in case of a tie. In general, his duties shall be such as devolve upon such an officer under approved parliamentary law, except as the same may be modified by these regulations.

SEC. 2. The Secretary shall attend all meetings of the Society and Board of Directors. He shall keep a record of the proceedings of the Society and the Board, which he shall transcribe in a book, to be authenticated by the Chairman as the transactions of the Society. He shall

receive and post proposals for membership, and
keep the accounts, documents and papers of the
Society in such manner and for such purposes as
the Board may appoint; he shall receive the con-
tributions, fines and other payments due to the
Society, and at the close of every meeting pay
the same to the Treasurer. The Secretary shall,
on all occasions, in the execution of his office, act
under the superintendence, control and direction of the Board, except as otherwise provided
in these regulations.

SEC. 3. The Treasurer shall be responsible
for such sums of money as may from time to
time be paid into his hands by the Secretary, or
by any person on account of the Society. He
shall also discharge any other functions relating
to the receipts and payments of the Society which
the Board may direct. He shall render his cash
account to the Board weekly; and he shall, before
taking upon himself the execution of his office,
give such security to the Board of Directors as
they shall think necessary.

SEC. 4. The Board of Directors shall have
control of all business carried on by the Society,
the employment of all necessary service or
work done for or on account of the Society; the
appointment and removal of the salesmen or
other employes necessary for conducting the
business, and may assign to any officers of the
Society such duties and salaries as they may
think fit, subject to the approval of the quarterly
meetings. The Board of Directors shall meet at
least once a week, and a majority shall be necessary to constitute a quorum for the transaction
of business, and all acts and orders done in such
Board meeting, within the powers delegated by
these rules, shall have the like force and effect as
if they were the acts and orders of the members,
at a general meeting thereof. Any member of
the Board not present within fifteen minutes of
the hour of meeting shall be fined. For their
services they shall receive such compensation as
the quarterly meeting may determine. Any five
of the Directors may call a special meeting of the

Society by giving three days' clear notice to the Secretary, in writing; but at such special meeting no other business than that specified in the notice shall be considered. All contracts authorized by the Board shall be signed by the President and countersigned by the Secretary. The Secretary shall keep a record of those present at each meeting of the Board.

SEC. 5. The Board of Directors shall cause a statement of the accounts of the Society, with all necessary vouchers, up to the last day in the months of March, June, September and December in each year, to be made out and laid before the Auditors not less than five days before each quarterly meeting; and it shall be the duty of the Auditors to examine the same, and lay before each such quarterly meeting a balance sheet, signed by the Auditors, showing the receipts and expenditures, and the assets and liabilities of the Society, and also the balance standing to the credit of each member, together with a statement of the affairs of the Society since the last quarterly meeting, and of its then condition.

Article V.—Meetings.

SECTION 1. The general meetings of the Society shall be held on the second Tuesday evening of each month. The meeting in January shall be considered the general annual meeting for the election of officers; the meetings in April, July and October shall be considered the quarterly meetings.

SEC. 2. Special meetings may be called by the Board, or on petition of fifteen members, three days clear notice to be given. Such calls shall clearly set forth the object of the special meeting, and no other business shall be transacted.

SEC. 3. Fifteen members shall constitute a quorum at any meeting. Each member shall have but one vote. Proxy votes shall not be allowed.

APPENDIX.

WOMAN'S WORK IN CO-OPERATION.

IN CO-OPERATION WOMAN HAS FOUND HER TRUE
SPHERE AND FIELD OF WORK.

Through co-operation she has been enabled to understand the inestimable value and importance of the principle as a factor in making home what it should be. Co-operation has not only made it possible, but practicable, for her to say :
"My Home to Me a Kingdom Is."
Less than sixteen years ago, when the Co-Operative Congress of 1883 met at Oxford, a few earnest women, who thought there was something that Woman might do to aid Co-Operation, came together and organized the Women's Co-Operative Guild.

It required but a short time to demonstrate its necessity and justifying its existence.

The organization has now about 240 branches, with a membership rising 12,000, mostly distributed throughout England and Scotland.

The following essay by a member of the Guild indicates the direction in which lies Woman's work in the movement, from a woman's standpoint:

AN ESSAY LESSON IN CO-OPERATION.

From "Woman's Corner" in *The Co-Operative News*, January 14, 1899.——

"There are two branches of co-operation—distributive and productive, and happily there is little need to say much now-a-days about the former, so great has been its success; its principles have become so well known and understood. But in case there are those amongst us who have not identified themselves much with the movement (and I think one of the principles of the Guild is to invite all to join and if they are not co-operators to try and make co-operators of them,) perhaps a little explanation here would enable them to understand more clearly what I am talking about. Therefore, I would just say that distributive co-operation consists for the most part of buying our goods at wholesale prices and selling them over the counter at retail or market price, taking care in the first instance to get as near the producer as possible, and distributing the profits to the consumers or purchasers just in proportion as they have the will and the power to support the stores — those receiving the most who buy the most. Thus it is made to appear that the more you eat, the more you get; which remark, strictly speaking, does not only apply to eatables, but also to the numerous other purchases you make, such as boots and shoes, clothing, drapery, coal, furniture — everything, in fact, you can be supplied with. This is distributive co-operation.

Now, productive co-operation means having mills, workshops, farms, etc., of our own, and instead of coming as near the producer as possible, actually manufacturing and producing our own goods, so doing away with all middlemen, and thereby reaping a double advantage. Now, a great deal may be said on productive co-operation, but I will leave that for several other members of our Guild to take up some other time, and for the little I have to say, will fall back on the distributive branch.

Poor people who have the good sense to make their purchases at the stores, taking care at the same time to see that their society is well and economically managed — one very important thing—will have acquired a power of improving their circumstances without any trouble, the advantages of which, in this early stage of the movement, it is difficult to fully or adequately tell. Some of the advantages, however, are too potent to escape notice and should be placed before as many of our friends as possible. One is, the greater the number of co-operators, the greater is the amount of good that co-operation is doing:

Firstly. On joining the society a member is no longer in fear of adulteration, of short weight, or of any of the numerous forms of deception which used to be so frequently and extensively practiced. Co-operation has very largely put an end to these evils by always demanding genuine goods.

Secondly. A new co-operator becomes, perhaps for the first time in his or her life, a shareholder in something real or substantial. He has a stake in the country and though he may not be a Conservative, he soon begins to feel and to think he has something to conserve. His little investment has grown while he has been asleep, and he finds that it still continues to grow, according to his co-operative loyalty. So much has been said for the domestic and pecuniary advantages of co-operation, that we not now dwell on the rescue from debt that it has bestowed on hundreds and thousands of its members. There is no need in its circle for the greasy book, as we have often heard it called, nor any fear at the week's end to pay for certain little items entered therein which cannot be accounted for. Neither need we dwell on the powerful influences for good that its exercises upon the minds and circumstances of it followers. Suffice it to say, then, that in co-operation we have a remedy for poverty, a good prospect for old age and an incentive to a higher moral life, which brings its reward in the present and will secure the praise of posterity."

All information in relation to the Women's Co-operative Guild may be obtained by addressing Miss Llewellyn Davis, Kirkby Lonsdale, Westmoreland, England.

ERATTA.

Page 17, line 7, add "too" after "benefits" and "confidence;" to read:

"benefits too well known and confidence too well grounded."

- Page 19, R. J. "Hinton," not "Hilton."

Page 19, 4th line from bottom, greatest trading body "in it," not "extant."

Page 22, line 18, add, "health" after "public," "public health and morals."

Page 23, line 33, "pure and unadulterated," not "adulterated."

Page 66, (head line) An "Easy," not "Essay" Lesson in Co-Operation.